BROOKLANDS COLLEGE LIBRARY
D0190269

The History and Techniques of The Great Masters

Pissarro

THE HISTORY AND TECHNIQUES
OF THE GREAT MASTERS

PISSARRO

Patricia Seligman

TIGER BOOKS INTERNATIONAL
LONDON

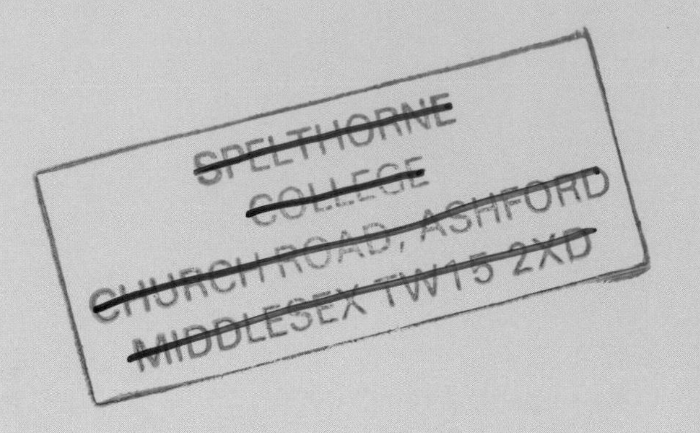

A QUARTO BOOK

This edition published by
Tiger Books International Ltd
3, Friars Lane,
Richmond,
Surrey, TW9 1NL

ISBN 1 85501 010 0

This book was designed and produced by
Quarto Publishing plc
The Old Brewery, 6 Blundell Street
London N7 9BH

Project Editor Hazel Harrison
Designer Carole Perks
Picture Researcher Katherine Russell-Cobb

Art Director Moira Clinch
Editorial Director Carolyn King

Typeset by Aptimage Limited
22 Clinton Place, Seaford, East Sussex BN25 1NP
Manufactured in Hong Kong by Regent
Publishing Services Limited
Printed in Hong Kong by Leefung-Asco
Printers Ltd

Contents

The Paintings

Introduction

"Remember that I have the temperament of a peasant, I am melancholy, harsh and savage in my works." With these words Camille Pissarro tried to explain his single-minded search for truth in all that he painted. "It is only in the long run that I can expect to please," he continued, "and then only those who have a grain of indulgence." Pissarro's dedication to his work, his family, his friends and his radical political beliefs caused him to choose an arduous route through life, which often found him in opposition to establishment views. Yet his solid good sense and the strength of his beliefs inspired loyalty amongst his friends — fellow painters, literary men and political thinkers — who regarded him as a patriarchal figure, a view no doubt prompted by his upright bearing and flowing beard, grey from his early forties. His role in the Impressionist and Neo-Impressionist movements (see page 13) was less that of the great man of ideas than that of the good counseller and appeaser, whose moral strength and good sense helped to rationalize the aims of the group.

CAMILLE PISSARRO
Self-Portrait
1873, Musée d'Orsay, Paris

Pissarro's strengths and weaknesses are poignantly revealed in the correspondence with his eldest son Lucien, living in London from 1883. These letters recount his daily dealings with all those involved in his life and work. We hear of his extensive family, so important to him, and his reactions to his friends and their work. All the characters of Parisian cultural life are there — among them artists Claude Monet, Paul Cézanne and Paul Gauguin; and writers and critics Emile Zola, Théodore Duret and J.-K. Huysmans — and many more. We are kept abreast of the political situation and informed of Pissarro's opinions; we witness his continual reassessment of the aims and methods of his art, and we follow his laboured progress towards recognition and financial stability.

Early life

The man who was to become an influential figure among the avant garde of Paris in the second half of the nineteenth century spent much of his formative years on a tiny island, that of St Thomas in the Virgin Islands, then a Danish colony. There he was born in 1830, son of a Jewish father and a Creole mother, and his childhood was spent in the small capital port of Charlotte Amalie, where his father was a merchant. His parents were ardently francophile, and sent their son over to Paris to school at the Savary Academy in Passy, where he would have had an opportunity to visit museums and to get to know the established masters of French art. According to later family accounts, Monsieur Savary gave him a traditional grounding in drawing and painting and implored his talented pupil on his return to St Thomas to draw the coconut palms from nature — a piece of advice that the young Pissarro duly followed.

It would appear that he returned to St Thomas with artistic ambitions, which did not meet with parental approval. His father found work for him in the family business checking cargo, where it is said he took every opportunity to practise his drawing skills. When he was twenty-one he took matters into his own hands, leaving his family and job with nothing but a note of farewell and sailing to Venezuela with a Danish artist, Fritz Melbye. In Caracas, the two young artists shared a studio for two years, establishing the first of many reciprocal artistic relationships which punctuated Pissarro's life. Drawings survive from this early period which testify to Pissarro's facility as a draughtsman. Fine sketches, and more finished wash drawings and watercolours, demonstrate a confidence in his medium and a developed style in part influenced by drawing manuals on techniques available at the time. In Caracas, he drew everything around him: landscapes, village scenes and sketchbooks full of figures — inside playing at cards or dancing outside in the market, fetching water and washing clothes.

The few extant paintings from this time, some of the local people, others light-filled tropical views, although competent, show a more orthodox approach to composition and style, generally attributed to the influence of Melbye who trained at the Copenhagen Academy of Fine Arts. The strictures of academic demands, as is so often the case, can be seen to eradicate the life and spontaneity of his drawing. Fortunately, such worries did not crush the will of young Pissarro who determined to pursue his artistic career. After returning briefly to St Thomas, Pissarro decided to sail for Paris to continue his studies under Melbye's brother Anton.

Paris and new influences

It is difficult to imagine how Pissarro must have reacted to the seething cauldron of ideas represented by Paris at this time. His direct approach and easy way with people as well as his innate intelligence must have helped with his integration into the life of the capital, but he did not immediately launch himself into the truant ideologies of the avant-garde. He began, indeed, by doing quite the opposite, striving in his thorough way to meet the standards of the Salon, the official body whose academic traditions dominated French artistic life. Until later in the century, the Salon was the only art marketplace, and even artists who were beginning to criticize its views as outmoded would submit works to the Salon Committee each year. As Anton Melbye's assistant, Pissarro settled down to working in the prescribed manner, producing the sizeable and carefully planned oil paintings demanded by the committee. In 1859, to the delight of his father, his first painting was accepted and exhibited.

Those works that have survived from the period before 1865 certainly show Pissarro's debt to Camille Corot and the Barbizon School – particularly Daubigny, Courbet and Millet – whose work he first fully appreciated on his arrival in Paris at the Great Exhibition of 1855. He is said to have called on Corot soon after this and later, after taking private lessons at the Ecole des Beaux Arts, became his pupil. As an old man, Pissarro looked back to "Claude Lorraine, Corot, the whole 18th century and Chardin especially" as early influences. He and Corot shared a love of rural scenes, painted from nature, which Pissarro, like his master, learnt to interpret with an underlying geometrical structure. But Corot's vision of landscape was principally idealized and sometimes stylized, and even though he painted with his easel set up in the countryside, he would work up his pictures in the studio into something which accorded with his preconceptions. A comparison of Corot's *Dardagny, Morning* of 1853 with Pissarro's *View from Louveciennes* of 1870 shows how alike the two artists appeared in their depiction of the countryside, but closer inspection reveals a fundamental difference between them. Corot is painting an image of arcadian bliss, whereas Pissarro's road is completely factual – rutted and edged with a sprawling hotchpotch of bushes, mounds of earth and trees in various stages of development. To contemporary viewers this streak of honesty in Pissarro was regarded as vulgar, the equivalent of a painter today including the rubbish and beer cans found on the side of a road.

Pissarro's desire to paint the countryside as he saw it, making it look real and without artifice, inevitably caused a rift between master and pupil. In 1859, at the free school, the Académie Suisse, Pissarro met a group of like-minded painters, among them Claude Monet and later Armand Guillaumin and Paul Cézanne. This younger generation of artists discussed their dissatis-

CHARLES FRANÇOIS DAUBIGNY
Alders
1872, National Gallery, London

In many ways Daubigny anticipated the work of the Impressionists, showing something of the immediate, sketch-like quality for which they were criticized. Pissarro would have first seen this work, along with those by other painters of the Barbizon school, at the Universal Exhibition in 1855, the same year that he arrived in Paris. Although he was initially more attracted to Corot's style, he was later to appreciate Daubigny's strong colours and bold brushwork.

CAMILLE COROT
Dardagny Morning
National Gallery, London

Pissarro particularly admired a painting by Corot that he saw at the Universal Exhibition of 1855. He found the imaginary landscape "the stuff of dreams," but it seems that his own desire to render landscape more truthfully could not accommodate the poetic approach. The two artists eventually parted company, but Corot's influence can be found in almost every aspect of Pissarro's early painting.

faction with the stranglehold of the official Salon, and Pissarro also found that his political views, centred on the importance of the individual, truth to nature and an abhorrence of artifice and false grandeur, coincided to an extent with the more fundamentally artistic aims of the group. In 1863 so many works were rejected by the Salon that Napoleon III ordered that the paintings turned away should be exhibited separately in an exhibition called the Salon des Refusés. Both Pissarro and Cézanne were included, but the show was dominated by the howls of protest over Manet's *Déjeuner sur l'Herbe.* The art establishment was as hostile to the show as the public, and it was not repeated, but it weakened the position of the Salon and established the notion of an alternative.

In the catalogues for the Salon exhibitions of 1865 and 1866, Pissarro acknowledges his debts to Anton Melbye and Corot, whom he cites jointly as his masters. But, by 1868, a more individual style had evolved and, recognizing this, Pissarro declared himself independent by citing no master in the catalogue. After visiting the 1868 exhibition and viewing Pissarro's two landscapes, Emile Zola, author and critic and champion of the new art, declared "Camille Pissarro is one of the three or four true painters of this day . . . I have rarely encountered a technique that is so sure." Certainly, his works of this time still owe much to Corot and to the naturalism and expressive brushwork of Courbet but his work is showing the early signs of an approach to painting which in the following decade is labelled "Impressionism".

At the beginning of the 1860s Pissarro accepted a new role, that of the family man. He met and formed a relationship with his mother's maid Julie Vellay, a vinegrower's daughter from Burgundy, later (in 1871) to become his wife. In 1863, his son Lucien was born, the first of a rambling family of seven children to whom Pissarro was a fond and loving father. In 1866 he, Julie and their small son established themselves at Pontoise outside Paris, later moving to Louveciennes. The countryside around the village, the river and woods became the inspiration for his painting in these years, but he retained a studio in Paris and kept in touch with developments in the city, occasionally attending Zola's "Thursdays" and also meetings with Monet, Renoir, Cézanne and Bazille at the Café Guerbois, where they worked towards a manifesto for their new art.

London

In 1870 the peace of Louveciennes was shattered by the news of the outbreak of the Franco-Prussian war. Pissarro, who still held Danish nationality, and was therefore unable to fight, was forced to remove his family to safety, eventually taking refuge in London with his half-sister. He begrudged his forced exile, but soon settled down to continue his work, painting his surroundings in Norwood where he stayed, then a fast-urbanizing village outside the city, not unlike Pontoise. *Lordship Lane Station, Dulwich,* painted at this time, records the effects of urbanization on the landscape — the railway and the new terraces of red-brick houses. Writing home in 1871 to his friend and patron Théodore Duret he sadly records: "My painting doesn't catch on, not at all, a fate that pursues me more or less everywhere."

Possibly the most important incident of his London stay was his introduction to the Parisian art dealer Paul Durand-Ruel, who was to help sell Pissarro's work throughout most of his life. Durand-Ruel put him in touch with Monet, also in London to escape the war, and together they viewed the work of Constable and Turner. Pissarro later remarked that although these British landscape artists certainly influenced them — what was more important, they provided confirmation that they were working in the right direction, particularly with respect to painting in the open air, the depiction of light and the fugitive effects of light and atmosphere. Whether through the influence of the British painters or as a result of his close contact with Monet, Pissarro's paintings of this period reflect a lighter, brighter palette. The paint is applied more freely, with loosely blended brushstrokes of colour and areas of impasto.

Pissarro and the Impressionists

Pissarro returned to Louveciennes to find that, during his absence, his home had been requisitioned as a slaughterhouse and his canvases torn from their stretchers and spread over the muddy ground in the garden to protect Prussian uniforms. After this desecration, they were thrown out onto the manure heap, where Pissarro found them. Only forty out of 1500 paintings covering twenty year's work remained, apart from the few he had sold, a tragedy which makes it difficult to assess his artistic progress up to this date. What remain are primarily landscapes in the Corot style — undoubtedly his more popular works. Most important among the casualties were his early paintings — documenting the birth of Impressionism, such as those painted in 1869 at La Grenouillère with Monet and Renoir. Also lost were no doubt his more informal paintings, portraits of his family and flower studies similar to his *Pink Peonies* of 1873 (page 27) and *Mme Pissarro Sewing Near a Window* of 1879 (see page 39).

But Pissarro quickly settled back into his former way of life, centred around his family, his work and his friends. Soon he was embroiled in discussions with his artist friends, including Monet, Manet, Renoir and Degas, on ways of providing an alternative to the Salon, which would enable them to exhibit and sell their work. In 1873 the Société Anonyme des Artistes, Peintres, Sculpteurs et Graveurs was set up as a joint stock company with fifteen artists with equal rights: Pissarro based the charter on the contract of the Pontoise bakers' union. His involvement in this group of artists is regarded as pivotal. Although he did not have the personal magnetism or the high-flying ideas of Monet, who could be seen as the guiding force, his well-respected strength and honesty did much to get things organized and hold the group together. The sombre self-portrait painted at this time shows a man with a prematurely grey beard, looking somewhat older than his forty-three years: it is little wonder that the group regarded him as a wise elder and father figure.

The fruit of these labours was the first Impressionist Exhibition, held in 1874. The critical reaction to it is well known, but it is easy to forget what exactly it was that so horrified the critics. Firstly they found fault with the subject matter. The paintings admired by the Salon committee were mainly religious, historical or mythological scenes, but here were "vulgar, commonplace" scenes of street people going about their everyday lives, or in Pissarro's case, the countryside as it really was — muddy, dirty and unkempt. Secondly, the manner of painting

CAMILLE PISSARRO
View from Louveciennes
1870, National Gallery, London

This painting, done just before Pissarro and his family fled to London to escape the Franco-Prussian War, shows close links with his former mentor Corot. Further observation, however, reveals a more down-to-earth vision of nature. Unlike Corot, Pissarro insisted on painting what he saw — in this case a hodge-podge of trees, bushes and mounds of earth along the country lane. Emile Zola said of Pissarro that "He is neither a poet nor a philosopher but simply a naturalist."

was found wanting by the traditionalists of the Beaux Arts school. They considered the pictures sketchy, like studies rather than finished works, with none of the qualities they saw as a *sine qua non* for good painting, such as academic organization of the composition or painstaking build up of paint layers over an underpainting. Instead, the paint was often applied wet-in-wet, one brushload of paint applied into another, and the painting finished in one sitting. The expressive use of the paint, with brushstrokes visible on the picture surface, became part of the vocabulary of this group of painters, but the academics considered this an effrontery to the painter's craft; they expected a work to testify to weeks, if not years, of labour. Finally, the "impressionist" painters shocked their critics with their new theories on colour, particularly those used for shadows which they saw as modified by the reflected light of surrounding objects. But there were, however, some enlightened critics, including Emile Zola, who braved public outcry and praised the new art.

Pissarro showed five landscapes in this exhibition. These may have appeared tame in comparison with some of the other entries, such as those by Monet or Manet — as he later said of his paintings "Whoever is in a hurry will not stop for me" — but he was described by the critic Armand Silvestre as "basically the inventor of this [Impressionist] painting". Indeed his expressive brushwork and his approach to colour shocked spectators, and were to continue doing so. In 1876 Albert Wolf in *Le Figaro* whined: "Try to make M Pissarro understand that trees are not violet, that sky is not the colour of fresh butter, that in no country do we see the things he paints and that no intelligence can accept such aberrations." Pissarro was painting everyday aspects of the countryside and, under the influence of Monet, he was already

CAMILLE PISSARRO
Hoar Frost, the Old Road to Ennery, Pontoise
1873, Musée d'Orsay, Paris

One of five paintings exhibited by Pissarro at the first Impressionist exhibition in 1874, this painting clearly justifies his place in the group. The strong diagonals of the road and the ploughed furrows highlighted with frost are crossed by the shadows of a row of trees outside the picture, an innovative compositional device that did not find favour with the contemporary critic A. J. Castagnary.

by the late 1860s applying the paint loosely in unblended brushstrokes of colour. His palette had become lighter and clearer, and in his pictures of this time small specks of red and viridian are left unmixed on the surface of the painting. In later years Cézanne was to refer to him as "the first Impressionist".

Friend and teacher

Pissarro's single-minded approach to his art may have something to do with the fact that, certainly in his early years, he found painting difficult. He was constantly searching for a solution to his methods of representing nature and this allowed him to reassess his work in the light of those around him. Back in Pontoise from 1872, he painted regularly with Cézanne, who, Lucien recalled later, often walked the three kilometres from Auvers-sur-Oise to join Pissarro. In a reappraisal of Courbet, both artists were exploring ways of representing space and unifying the painting, and there is evidence of a reciprocal exchange of ideas. Cézanne wanted to study the countryside through Pissarro's eyes, and was particularly interested in Pissarro's Pontoise landscapes of the late '60s, where he first built up areas with refined blocks of colour. Pissarro reassessed these developments, deliberately imitating the style of Cézanne, as in *The Little Bridge at Pontoise* of 1875 (see page 31). The two artists worked together from nature in the surrounding countryside, using the palette knife to help them broaden their approach and refine the composition to zones of colour.

Cézanne, although not much younger than Pissarro, said of him that "he was a father for me. A man to consult and a little like the good Lord." Many of Pissarro's friends write in a similar vein; even Lucien, who was taught at home by his father, described him as a "splendid teacher, never imposing his personality on his pupil." Gauguin, who worked more with him at the end of the '70s, and who was greatly influenced by his peasant-girl studies of the early '80s, refers to him as "one of my masters," and the American Impressionist Mary Cassatt noted that he was "such a teacher that he could have taught the stones to draw correctly." Not only did he influence his own contemporaries but the next generation of artists too — particularly Henri Matisse and Francis Picabia.

As the decade progressed, Pissarro struggled more and more with his technique. After the mid-1870s he adopted a comma-like brushstroke to express himself, creating form and tone out of hatched and cross-hatched areas of small strokes, which built up to a textured impasto surface. *Kitchen Garden with Trees in Flower, Pontoise* of 1877 (see page 35) shows his early attempts with this new approach. Some of his canvases of this period became overloaded with superimposed strokes of thick paint, creating a densely painted, almost sculpted

CAMILLE PISSARRO
Two Female Harvesters
1890, Ashmolean Museum, Oxford

Pissarro was a skilful and prolific draughtsman from his youth, when he had spent his time drawing the cargo-handlers in the port of Charlotte Amalie in the Virgin Islands. He used his drawings to record visual information which he would later incorporate into his paintings. This drawing in black chalk was among the careful preparations for a tempera painting, *The Harvesters*, shown in the seventh Impressionist Exhibition.

CAMILLE PISSARRO
The Pea-Pickers
1890, Ashmolean Museum, Oxford

This vibrant gouache of peasant women planting pea sticks is one of a number of fans Pissarro painted from 1879 onwards. It is very different from the earthiness of his earlier paintings. The rhythmic curves of the figures impart something of the quality of a ritual dance to their arduous task, and the pale, luminous colours seem to conspire in distancing the scene from reality. A painting by Pissarro of the same composition was owned by Monet.

paint surface. At times the technique achieved a depth of colour and a sense of form which can only be appreciated in the original. Close to, the paint is thick and sometimes smeared and matted; standing back, however, the pigments fuse and forms appear. By degrees, a painting of great penetration emerges. But Pissarro was unhappy with his work, feeling that it lacked clarity and structure.

Perhaps in reaction to these difficulties, Pissarro explored other media. A particularly successful venture was undertaken with Degas to publish a journal of original prints. The result of their partnership was a large group of fine etchings by both artists, exploring unconventional ways of creating texture and depicting light. Another new scheme, possibly inspired by Degas, was the decoration of fans. Painted in gouache and watercolour on silk or linen, Pissarro seemed to want to explore the effect of the shape on the composition and also the capabilities of the new medium. *Le Repas Champêtre,* painted later, in 1891, shows a charming scene of a harvesting picnic. The bleaching light of the midday sun contrasts with the subtleties of colour and tone in the shade, which Pissarro captures with delicate hatching strokes of pure colour.

New themes and Neo-Impressionism

Perhaps in an effort to break out of what he considered a stylistic mire, Pissarro in the 1880s boldly explored new themes and new ways of expressing them. He was not alone in his stylistic dilemma: the same feeling of dissatisfaction, and perhaps stagnancy after the initial excitement of the early Impressionist years, was also being experienced by other members of the Impressionist group. Pissarro turned back to a theme which had always concerned him – the life of country people. It was not a new subject for him – his drawings, from his early Caracas market scenes, are peppered with sketches of women working the land. But in the early 1880s it is as if Pissarro focused in on the peasants in his country scenes and his attention is drawn to scenes such as the two female harvesters of 1882 shown here.

Similar scenes by François Millet must have influenced Pissarro, who shared his socialist beliefs, but Degas summed up the fundamental difference between them: "Millet? His *Sower* is sowing for Mankind. Pissarro's peasants are working to make a living." Pissarro had been reading anarchist literature since the 1860s, particularly works by P-J Proudhon, who encouraged painters to educate the public by painting people at work or at home as they were in reality, without idealizing their lives. Even in his earliest drawings, executed in St Thomas and Caracas, Pissarro had shown a fascination for the daily lives of the blacks and South American Indians, which he recorded with honest simplicity, so Proudhon's words must have struck a chord with him.

The overthrow of the Paris Commune in 1871, followed by the execution or exile of many supporters, decimated French left-wing politics, but at this time Pissarro, unlike Courbet who was exiled, was not involved. It was not until the 1880s, when the Anarchist movement gained strength and became more active, that Pissarro's views evidently began to harden. In 1882,

CAMILLE PISSARRO
View from my Window, Eragny-sur-Epte
1886-88, Ashmolean Museum, Oxford

This fresh yet restrained view of the artist's garden from an upstairs window was painted at the height of his Neo-Impressionist phase. Like Seurat and Signac, he built up his paintings with dabs of pure colour that were intended to mix optically in the eye of the viewer. In July 1886 he wrote about the painting to his son Lucien: "It appears that the subject is not popular. They [Durand-Ruel and his son] object to the red roof and the back yard, just what gives character to the painting."

Renoir referred to Pissarro as a revolutionary and alluded to his Anarchist sympathies by writing that it would not be long before Pissarro invited the Russian Lavrof (a known anarchist) to exhibit with them. However, Pissarro seldom overtly used his art to preach a political message even though his sympathetic treatment of country people and his preference for more humble subject matter made his position clear. It is no accident that the châteaux at Pontoise and Louveciennes are never included in his rural views.

Pissarro's paintings of country figures, particularly peasant girls, in the first half of the 1880s, break new ground in terms of their spatial organization. He places the figure in an enclosed setting, preventing any recession into the picture space and thus focusing attention on the figure, which is treated more like a portrait. In *The Shepherdess* (see page 43) the wistful young girl is depicted against a backdrop of generalized foliage which spreads out like a tapestry behind her. In this peasant girl series Pissarro perfects the painting style he was working towards in the late 1870s, covering the canvas with a consistent network of small brushstrokes.

In the light of both the unified brushwork and his use of pure strokes of colour in these paintings, his conversion to Neo-Impressionism later in the decade seems a less radical step. In 1884 Pissarro met Seurat and Signac, two young artists who had been working towards a new "scientific" based theory for art, based on treatises by theorists, among them Charles Henry, Ogden Rood and David Sutter. These painters set out to use pure pigments — no earth colours or black — premixed on the palette as set out in Hayet's colour wheel shown on page 15. Shades of colour and tone were built up by placing small patches, or dots, of pure colour side by side, to be blended optically by the eye.

Pissarro's search for a more structured method of painting had also led him to Henry and Rood, so he was excited by Seurat's interpretation. In addition, the Neo-Impressionists, like Pissarro, supported the Anarchist cause, which was reflected in their theory. With typical industry, he threw himself into mastering the new techniques, but the system was time-consuming and laborious. From 1885 to 1888 he struggled with its limitations, producing some inspired examples of Neo-Impressionism, including *View from My Window, Eragny* and *Apple Picking at Eragny-sur-Epte* (see page 55), both painted in 1888. Later, in 1896, he explained in a letter to Henry Van de Velde, the Belgian designer, how insensitive he found the system, making it impossible for him to follow his fleeting sensations and to give his work a sense of movement and life. It would appear that he also found the system created the very sense of artifice in his art which he had always avoided, making it difficult to record what were to him the all important transient details of nature.

CAMILLE PISSARRO
Bedford Park, The Old Bath Road
1897, Ashmolean Museum, Oxford

This painting was begun, but not completed, during Pissarro's last visit to London to see his ailing son Lucien. Being unfinished, it shows how he built up his paintings: clearly visible are the blue lines of the underdrawing, done quickly and freely in dilute paint to map out the main components of the composition. The top part of the picture, with the red brickwork, is more finished, but the figures in the foreground are still at an early stage, as is the hedge, which has been built up with broad strokes of different greens applied from all directions.

Final years

Pissarro's later years were dogged by a recurring eye infection but this physical affliction in no way stopped him painting. In effect, it meant that he was no longer able to work outside, except in warm weather, and this turn of events encouraged him to reappraise both his working methods and his subject matter. A trip to Rouen earlier in 1883, when he painted *The Quays at Rouen*, perhaps reminded him of the busy life of the port in the Virgin Islands where he spent his youth. Pissarro found the town very stimulating, painting a number of views from the shelter of a hotel room. It is not surprising therefore that, after the onset of the eye infection, he returned to similar urban/portside themes all painted from upper storey rented rooms. In his last years he produced series of paintings of the same urban view under different conditions of light and weather, returning to places and themes which had attracted the Impressionists in their early years. He moved around Northern France painting from hotel rooms in Rouen and Paris as well as Le Havre and Dieppe. He continued with the same urban themes when visiting London in the '90s to stay with Lucien in Chiswick, painting the Bank Holiday crowds at Kew and also painting the parks, as Monet had done earlier. In his later style he reverted to the highly worked canvases of the late '70s, often painting in forms of people or trees over the thickly built up impasto layer.

Contrary to what one might expect, Pissarro as he grew older became increasingly active in his support for the Anarchist movement. His support ranged from involvement with the Anarchist newspaper *La Révolte* to his backing of Zola in the Dreyfus Affair, which developed from a burst of anti-semitism in France in the late '90s. After the murder of the French President in 1894 by an Italian Anarchist, Pissarro as a known Anarchist sympathizer was forced to flee to Belgium, where he stayed for four months. Even two weeks before his death, he was still ready to demonstrate his loyalties by joining a pilgrimage to Médan on the first anniversary of Zola's death.

In his self-portrait of 1903 (see page 59), we see Pissarro a few months before he died, an upright, dignified old man still with a sense of vitality. He continued to work up until the last moment, in good weather pushing his patent easel on wheels around the orchard at Eragny. In the summer he even sold five canvases, including two to the local museum. A few months later, in November, he died, revered by his friends and fellow painters as a great artist and a good man. Signac wrote to Lucien: "He will always be for me *le vieux Maître*... he leaves behind him one of the most beautiful painting *oeuvres* of our times and the memory of a life of impeccable distinction and utter dignity."

Pissarro's Painting Methods

For outdoor work, Pissarro had a specially designed easel on wheels, which could be pushed along like a barrow until he found a suitable spot for a painting. Here he is seen with his wife Julie and two of his children, Paul-Emile and Jeanne (Cocotte). He is wearing his everyday working clothes — a loose jacket, wooden clogs (his country wear) and the wide-brimmed hat which seldom left his head.

Pissarro's palette and brushwork changed from one period of his career to another, but his general approach to his paintings was a constant factor. His philosophy of landscape painting is set out in a letter of about 1896 to a young painter.

"Look for the kind of nature that suits your temperament. The motif should be observed more for shape and colour than for drawing ... Precise drawing is dry and hampers the impression of the whole ... it is the brushstroke of the right value and colour which should produce the drawings ... Don't work bit by bit, but paint everything at once by placing tones everywhere, with brushstrokes of the right colour and value, while noticing what is alongside. Use small brushstrokes and try to put down your perceptions immediately ... Cover the canvas at the first go and then work until you see nothing more to add. Observe the aerial perspective well, from foreground to the horizon, the reflections of sky, of foliage. Don't be afraid of putting on colour, refine the work little by little. Don't proceed according to rules and principles, but paint what you observe and feel. Paint generously and unhesitatingly, for it is best not to lose the first impression. Don't be timid in the presence of nature; one must be bold at the risk of being deceived and making mistakes. One must have only one teacher — nature; she is the one always to be consulted."

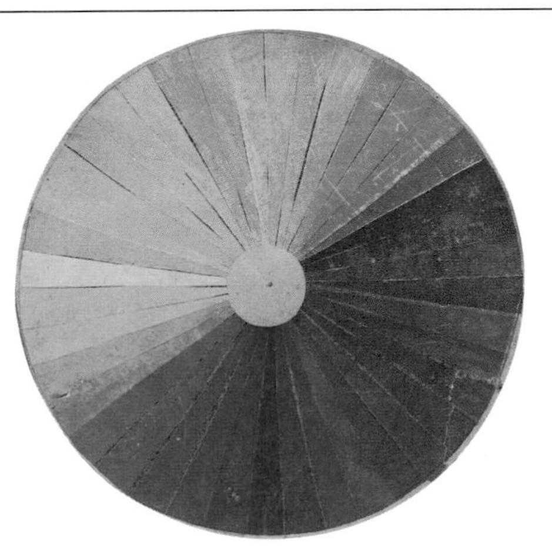

Louis Hayet, a friend of Pissarro, painted this colour circle based on Ogden Rood's colour wheel. Such charts were helpful to the Neo-Impressionist painters. For the idea of optical mixing to be really successful, colours had to be chosen with great care, the only hues premixed on the palette being those adjacent to one another on the circle.

The colours Pissarro used for *Apple Picking at Eragny-sur-Epte* were probably similar to those used by Seurat. These were cadmium yellow, vermilion, madder lake, cobalt violet, ultramarine, cobalt blue, cerulean blue, viridian, emerald (Veronese) green and cadmium yellow light.

CHRONOLOGY OF PISSARRO'S LIFE

1830 10 July — born on the island of St Thomas, Virgin Islands.

1842-7 At school in Passy outside Paris.

1847 Returns to St Thomas and joins family business.

1852-4 To Venezuela with Fritz Melbye, Danish painter.

1855 Travels to Paris. Visits World Exhibition.

1856-8 Works in Paris, with financial help from his parents.

1859 First picture accepted for Salon (exhibits in 1864, 1865, 1866, 1868, 1869 and 1870). Visits Académie Suisse, where he meets Monet.

1860 Meets Julie Vellay, later his wife.

1861 Registers as a copyist at the Louvre. Meets Guillaumin and Cézanne at the Académie Suisse.

1863 Three landscapes exhibited in the Salon des Refusés. Son Lucien born.

1866 Settles at Pontoise. Attends Zola's meetings and formative meetings of the Impressionist group at the Café Guerbois.

1867 Paints *View of l'Hermitage at Pontoise.*

1869 Moves to Louveciennes. Paints with Monet and Renoir at La Grenouillère.

1870 Franco-Prussian War drives Pissarro to London.

1871 Marries Julie. Paints *Lordship Lane Station, Dulwich,* London. Returns to Louveciennes.

1872 Settled back in Pontoise. Cézanne at Auvers-sur-Oise.

1873 Impressionist Society formed. Paints *Pink Peonies.*

Pink Peonies

Mme Pissarro Sewing Near a Window

The Shepherdess

1874 15 April exhibits five landscapes in the first Impressionist exhibition (Pissarro exhibits in all of them — 1876, 1877, 1879, 1880, 1881, 1882 and 1886).

1875-80 Struggling to make a living (fourth son born 1878). Paints *The Little Bridge, Pontoise* (1875) and *Kitchen Garden with Trees in Flower, Pontoise* (1877).

1879 About this time, paints *Mme Pissarro Sewing near a Window.* Gauguin paints with Pissarro at Pontoise.

1881 Break-up of original Impressionist group. Paints *The Shepherdess.*

1883 Durand-Ruel organizes a one-man show for Pissarro. Lucien leaves for England. Visit to Rouen, painting *The Quays at Rouen.*

1884 Moves to Eragny.

1885-91 Joins Seurat and Signac in the Neo-Impressionist movement.

1888 Paints *Apple Picking at Eragny-sur-Epte.* In September contracts eye infection.

1890 Visits Lucien in London (and again in 1892 and 1897).

1892 Successful one-man show of a hundred paintings. Buys the house at Eragny.

1894 To Belgium to escape reprisals against Anarchists.

1893-1903 Paints urban views of Rouen, Le Havre, Dieppe and Paris such as *The Boulevard Montmartre at Night,* 1897.

1903 13 November: Pissarro dies in Paris.

THE PAINTINGS

View of L'Hermitage at Pontoise

1867

$35^{7}/_{8} \times 59^{1}/_{4}$in/91×1.505m

Oil on canvas

Wallraf-Richartz Museum, Cologne

Pissarro is perhaps best known for peaceful rural scenes such as this, painted when he was living in the small village of Pontoise just outside Paris. He had moved there in his mid-thirties with Julie Vellay, later to be his wife, and their young son Lucien. Although Pissarro kept a studio in Paris to stay in touch with his artist and writer friends and to try and sell his work, he was more at ease in the countryside, which provided him with the inspiration for his work. This view, showing L'Hermitage in the north-east part of Pontoise, is one of a series painted at this time, all of them exploring methods of composition and ways of depicting light and space.

The early paintings of Pontoise are larger than much of Pissarro's other work, being painted to the specifications of the Salon committee, which laid down stringent rules about submissions for possible inclusion in the annual Salon exhibition. Following the traditions of the time, artists were expected to begin by making sketches and oil studies of their subject from life. This information was then worked up in the studio into a full-sized oil sketch, and finally the painting was executed in slow stages with painstaking care. Although Pissarro was soon to find himself in strong opposition to the old-fashioned and increasingly outdated aims and methods of the Salon, he was, like his contemporaries, forced to comply with them through a need to sell his work. He exhibited views of L'Hermitage, Pontoise, in the Salons of both 1868 and 1869. Of the two landscapes shown in 1868, Emile Zola, the writer and critic, wrote in highly complimentary terms. "The originality here is profoundly human. It is not derived merely from a facility of hand or from a falsification of nature. It stems from the temperament of the painter himself and comprises a feeling for truth resulting from an inner conviction." Even at this early stage, Zola, who was to become a close acquaintance of Pissarro's, had an uncanny grasp of what the artist was trying to achieve in his painting.

It was really only in the mid-'60s that Pissarro evolved a truly individual style, as represented by this work. The evenly cast light in the painting allows the forms to be defined without the descriptive use of cast shadows. By reducing the walls and roofs to clearly defined shapes and defining them with solid directional strokes of colour, the warren of buildings is boldly and unambiguously expressed. These early paintings were to provide an inspiration to Cézanne when the two artists worked together in Pontoise in the early 1870s.

Although the strong underlying geometric composition, with the small figures in the foreground, and the mute greens and brown earth colours, are reminiscent of Corot, the bold handling of the paint — both with hog's hair brushes and the palette knife — shows Pissarro's affinity with Courbet. He needed to use a well-loaded brush in this painting, as it covers another work underneath. In places the ridged brushstrokes of the painting beneath catch the light, working against those that are superimposed. The influence of Daubigny, who strongly supported the inclusion of Pissarro's work in the 1868 Salon, can also be seen in the lively working of the paint surface. But already there are signs of cross-fertilization between Pissarro and the younger artists later to form part of the Impressionist group, Monet and Manet particularly. Manet's *Déjeuner sur l'Herbe* had made a great impact on his circle after the outcry it created at the Salon des Refusés in 1863. One of the bitter criticisms levelled at it related to its "vulgar" or commonplace treatment of the subject, and the same complaint was also frequently made of Pissarro, who, it was considered, was unable to find anything elegant or poetic to paint in the countryside.

This painting is considered one of the most important works of Pissarro's early *oeuvre*. The underlying geometrical structure is a careful balance of horizontals – the vegetable patch in the foreground, the wall, the ridges of the roofs and the background brow of the hill – with strong, punchy diagonals leading the eye from the foreground on the right and repeated in the eaves of the buildings and the stripes of the landscape up on the hill behind. This structure holds the composition together on the picture surface, and is reinforced by the handling of the paint, which makes a consistent pattern of brushstrokes over the surface. The canvas, barely visible through the thick layers of paint, is an unusual chevron-woven twill. In paintings such as *Hoar Frost* (see page 10), the diagonal weave is used to enforce the composition. In size the canvas is close to the standard "marine 80" often used by Corot and recommended for paintings submitted to the Salon. Normally Pissarro preferred much smaller canvases which were easy to carry on painting trips in the countryside and quicker to complete before the light changed.

1

2

1 Pissarro was fond of the rather dull, even light usually cast on a grey day, which prevented high contrasts and deep shadows — he was later to find that the English climate could often provide him with these conditions. The sky area here has been applied in places wet-in-wet, with light lively strokes that give a sense of movement to what is otherwise a still scene. In places, as on the sky line, the pinkish tones of the underpainting are allowed to show through the broken brushwork, warming the cool greys of the sky area.

2 Pissarro was described by one critic as "a painter of cabbages." Certainly he appeared to delight in the sense of order achieved in a kitchen garden and the demonstration of good honest toil it afforded. Like Corot, he used figures in his early landscapes to give a sense of scale and often to enforce the vertical compositional lines. Here the line down the backs of the man's legs is a continuation of a clear vertical from the buildings and a chimney above, which helps to tie the foreground to the background. The eye is naturally drawn to this figure, painted in high contrast and remarkable economy. The same broad flat brush has been used as for the buildings. The waistband and trousers are given form by working ochre wet-in-wet into the dark umber below.

3

3 In this detail of the farm buildings in the left middle ground Pissarro's bold handling of the subdued earth colours forms an almost abstract composition of geometric shapes. The treatment of paint in this area of the painting shows the influence of Courbet and, in turn, was later to be a source of inspiration to Cézanne. Bold strokes leave the mark of a flat hog's hair brush in the thick juicy paint. These brushmarks help to enforce the different planes of the walls and roofs which are otherwise merely described in flat colours, sometimes clarified with broken outlines with a dry brush, as on the eaves. The slate-grey roof in the foreground has been applied with a palette knife, giving a smoother appearance to the paint. But note how the dark underpainting is allowed to show through around the edges to help define the outline.

Lordship Lane Station, Dulwich

1871

$17\frac{1}{2} \times 28\frac{1}{2}$in/44.5×72.5cm

Oil on canvas

Courtauld Institute Galleries, London

This scene of the newly built Lordship Lane Station, which served the crowds visiting exhibitions at Crystal Palace, was painted on Pissarro's first visit to London. In 1870 he brought his family to England to escape the Franco-Prussian War, and they stayed with his half-sister in Upper Norwood just outside the city. Pissarro had found himself in a difficult situation when the war broke out: he was unable to fight with the French as he still retained Danish nationality, and it soon became clear that his house at Louveciennes was in the path of the invading Prussians. Abandoning over 1500 paintings, the body of his early work, he first fled with his family to Montfoucault in Britanny to take refuge with his great friend, the painter Ludovic Piette, and from there in the autumn they travelled over to England.

Later in his life Pissarro was to visit London regularly, and he enjoyed it, but he begrudged this first visit, writing to his friend Théodore Duret in June 1871: "I am here for only a very short time. I count on returning to France as soon as possible . . . Here there is no art; everything is a question of business." Even so this London visit gave him a chance to reassess his work in the light of Constable and Turner, whom he viewed with Monet, also in London to escape the war.

The structure of the painting relies on a traditional compositional device, that of receding parallel lines which lead the eye into the picture space. Pissarro has effectively reversed the process, however, by depicting the train steaming towards the viewer, against the natural "entry" into the composition, but he ensures that the eye is taken back towards the rows of newly built houses on the left by using the fence, with its strong browns and blacks, to direct the way. Similarly the strong, swift grey line of paint on the brow of the bank prevents the eye from leaving the picture on the right.

The foreground of scrubland is an interesting area of paint, loosely executed in quick strokes in varying greens and browns. The movement here contrasts with the flat colour of the buildings in the background, which although not as important as those in *l'Hermitage, Pontoise* (see page 19), are treated in the same manner. Although the overall palette reflects the dull light of the day, the warm red-brown of the buildings is taken through the painting, and helps to unify it. This colour can be seen boldly painted into the green of the grass, in the tracks and on the train, and it is also worked in to modify the whites and greys of the sky and the impasto of the cloud of steam. But there are also small patches of pure colour which intensify the range of hues — a bright yellow in the grass on the right and vermilion painted wet-in-wet on the front of the steam engine.

Most of Pissarro's early paintings include small figures in the foreground, usually for compositional reasons and to help with the interpretation of scale. It is interesting that X-ray and infra-red photographs have shown a small figure standing in the foreground, on the bank to the right of the tracks, that Pissarro eventually painted out.

Pissarro painted this urban scene from a footbridge over the railway cutting to the south of Lordship Lane Station (now demolished), near Crystal Palace. His interest in recording what he saw as the threat of urbanization became an enduring theme in his later years. Turner's painting *Rain, Steam and Speed,* painted in 1844, would have been seen by Pissarro at the National Gallery, but even though they both depict an oncoming steam train, Pissarro's painting uses none of Turner's dramatic atmospheric effects. His own approach to nature is more humble.

Claude Monet
Hyde Park
1871, Museum of Art, Rhode Island School of Design

Also in London to escape the Prussian invasion of France, Monet met up with Pissarro, and together they viewed the Constables and Turners at the National Gallery. This view of Hyde Park painted at the time shows many similarities with Pissarro in style and colouration, although Monet's more "blonde" palette was to influence his friend.

1

2

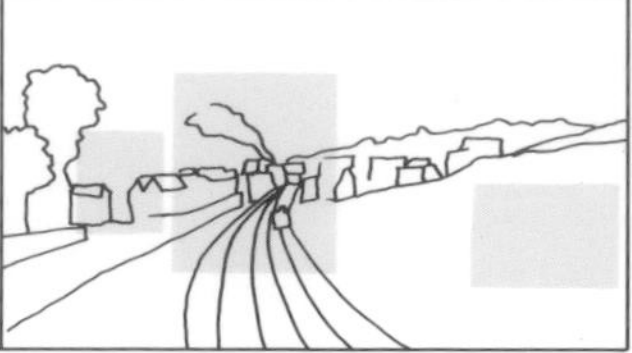

1 This perfectly conceived vignette in the left background demonstrates Pissarro's attention to detail. Although executed with small economic dabs of paint, the intentions of the artist are quite clear, and he has also been concerned with recession. The colours, though of a surprisingly bright hue, are well knocked back with white in accordance with atmospheric perspective. The glimpse of the distant road disappearing over the hill helps to take the eye further into the picture space. Tiny patches of the white canvas have been allowed to show through on the eaves of the red houses to give sparkling highlight effects.

2 At first sight the stretches of scrubland on either side of the railway track seem pointlessly barren; Pissarro's desire to produce an honest depiction of the scene would not allow him to compromise. But closer inspection shows a wide variation in the use of colour and technique in this area. Working in small dabs with probably a fairly soft brush, he has applied the paint in places wet-in-wet, leaving the colours unblended, while the darker green clumps of grass have been added with a dry brush. The result is a patchwork of colours with a wide range of greens, areas of browny red which tie in with the buildings in the background, and accents of pure yellow.

3

3 *Actual size detail* If Pissarro had wanted to produce a more dramatic composition, he would have focused in on the train as this detail does. But he was interested in other aspects of this scene — more particularly the way in which the recently built railway has carved this gentle landscape in half. As this detail shows, each element of the painting is treated separately: flat brushstrokes are used for the rows of houses, thick moulded impasto for the angry puff of steam, horizontal wet-in-wet dabs for the sky, and sweeping directional strokes for the railway lines. The cruciform signal silhouetted against the sky is added with a dry brush over the sky colour.

Pink Peonies

1873

$28\frac{3}{4} \times 23\frac{5}{8}$in/$73 \times 60$cm

Oil on canvas

Ashmolean Museum, Oxford

It is in informal paintings such as this depiction of peonies that Pissarro sometimes appears to come closest to mainstream Impressionism. His presentation of the subject matter would have appeared very unstructured at the time: the rather overblown flowers are captured in their natural state, seemingly unarranged and uncomposed, placed in what would certainly have been regarded as a commonplace pot. To our modern eyes, all these things add to the charm of the painting, but in the early 1870s the Salon would expect a flower painting to be a formal arrangement of blooms, with careful consideration given to shape, colour and technical execution. Pissarro's peonies would have contrasted with more fashionable drawing-room flower paintings by his contemporary and friend of the Impressionists Henri Fantin-Latour (1836-1904), whose graceful arrangements and perfect rose specimens, presented in cut glass or fine porcelain vases, were more acceptable to Parisian society.

In 1873 Pissarro was once again staying in rue l'Hermitage in Pontoise, painting mainly in the surrounding countryside. From this period there appear to be a greater number of informal paintings – similar subjects no doubt existed before 1870 but fell victim to the invading Prussian army. Still lifes and informal portraits of his family from this period are among some of his most charming paintings.

Pissarro has captured the essence of these opulent flowers with inspired, free-flowing strokes of juicy paint. But the paint surface is varied, being thin in places, with the white-primed canvas allowed to show through. Appropriately, the thickest paint is to be found on the blooms, and the eye is drawn to these, painted in impasto with the comma-like strokes that were later to become Pissarro's hallmark. The pale pinks are spiked with modified dashes of yellow, strong blue and vermilion, capturing the translucency of the petals. The leaves, on the other hand, are painted more thinly and broadly, with more concentration on the shape and pattern they make on the picture surface. The treatment of the vase and table is different again, with the paint used wet-in-wet, and broad strokes of a hog-hair brush following the form of the outline. Finally, the plain cream background is found on closer inspection to be a network of surface brushwork, with touches of pink from the peonies and green from the leaves worked into the main colour to help unify the painting.

Although the picture has the appearance of being spontaneous and uncomposed, it clearly has been carefully thought out. The vase is placed in the centre of the canvas, but this symmetry is tempered by the arrangement of the flowers, the positioning of the semi-circular table (possibly that in his portrait of his daughter Minette of the same time) and the subtle variation in the background colour. The surface tension is held by the repeating curves of the table, flowers, leaves and vase.

Flower paintings and still lifes were popular at the time that these full-blown peonies were painted. Indeed Pissarro's friend Monet at the end of the 1870s found he could sell such subjects more readily and for higher prices than his landscapes. This carefully conceived small painting, however, was obviously not meant for sale and in fact remained in Pissarro's family until bequeathed to the Ashmolean Museum by his son Lucien. Perhaps Pissarro captured the beauty of the flowers for his wife, Julie, who was very fond of her garden and at one time sent peony seeds to her sister-in-law in London. Pissarro only came back to painting flowers and still lifes much later on in his life, when he may perhaps have felt under less pressure to sell his work.

1

2

1 With broad strokes of a wide flat brush, Pissarro follows the contours of the simple vase. As we can see on the right side of the vase, the composition was first mapped out in charcoal on prepared canvas. Here the charcoal has mixed with the whitish paint of the vase to form a blurred outline.

2 This wonderfully rich pattern of strokes helps build up the reflections in the polished table — perhaps the folding gate-legged table shown in Pissarro's portrait of Minette of about the same time. Again he links up the elements of the painting through colour. Touches of the bright red-orange in the table can be found in the blooms, and the free strokes of green in the foliage. With more concern for the expressive nature of the brushwork than the accuracy of the elipse, the edge of the table is outlined with a bold stroke of the same red-orange enforced with blue-grey.

3 *Actual size detail* This luscious bloom of the palest pink is expressed in clear strokes of juicy paint. It appears that Pissarro used a smaller, softer brush for the blooms than for the rest of the painting. The paint has been applied wet-in-wet, working in the darker reds of the heart of the flower and then modifying these with strokes of pale pink impasto. Even so, touches of pure vermilion and almost pure Prussian blue can still be located. The comma-like strokes seen here were later used by Pissarro to cover whole canvases in a complex rhythm of strokes.

3 *Actual size detail*

The Little Bridge, Pontoise

1875

$25^{3}/_{4} \times 32^{1}/_{8}$in/65.5×81.5cm

Oil on canvas

Städtische Kunsthalle, Mannheim

In later years, Pissarro's son, Lucien, remembered how Cézanne used to trudge the three kilometres from his house in Auvers-sur-Oise to paint with Pissarro at Pontoise. There are photographs of the two of them setting out to paint in the countryside with their painting equipment in backpacks — in winter wearing warm hats, thick dark capes and walking boots, and in summer, straw hats to keep off the sun. The two worked closely together during the 1870s, learning from and inspiring each other. At the beginning Cézanne wanted to learn to observe nature in the same manner as Pissarro but, in the course of their work, their combined interests led them to more important developments. Both artists were reassessing the realism and expressive style of Courbet, whom they admired both as a painter and for his radical politics. A sensitive portrait of Cézanne by Pissarro of 1874 has been shown to express their political beliefs and includes a cartoon of Courbet in the background as well as a caricature from the leftist paper *l'Eclipse*.

Cézanne's influence is very obvious in *The Little Bridge, Pontoise,* but the style which Pissarro is imitating here was itself derived from Cézanne's study of Pissarro's earlier Pontoise series, so the influence is not all one-way. In those early paintings, such as *l'Hermitage, Pontoise* (see page 19), Pissarro had explored methods of representing spatial depth, particularly in the architecture, through interlocking zones of flat paint. Here, under Cézanne's influence, he applies the same method overall to the full range of subject matter and particularly to nature, by simplifying forms, colours and tones.

To produce these flat areas of paint, both artists worked with large palette knives, which also helped to broaden their approach; Lucien Pissarro remembered a package arriving from Paris containing two large knives for his father and his friend. Although Pissarro had used a palette knife before, he had not considered using it over the whole picture surface. A comparison of Pissarro's painting with Cézanne's *Etang des Soeurs* of the same time (opposite below), shows that Pissarro's sensitivity to nature made it hard for him to reduce the composition to basic elements, as in doing so they lost their importance as natural forms. Consequently, although Pissarro learnt from Cézanne, he did not pursue this particular method. But these experiments of the early 1870s renewed his interest in the surface texture of paint and introduced the idea of a unifying approach to brushwork, which he went on to exploit in the late '70s and early '80s.

Pissarro's admiration for Cézanne's work never diminished. It was with Pissarro's support that Cézanne exhibited in the first Impressionist exhibition in 1874 and, as an old man, in 1895, Pissarro wrote to Lucien about Cézanne's show in Paris "in which there were exquisite things, still lifes of irreproachable perfection . . . landscapes, nudes and heads that are unfinished, but yet grandly conceived and so *painted,* so supple. Why? Sensation is there."

Painted at the height of Pissarro's close working relationship with Cézanne, *The Little Bridge, Pontoise* relates closely to a number of paintings by Cézanne of the same time, including *Etang des Soeurs, Osny* (below). Pissarro's sensitivity to the dappled light in this woodland scene has led him to use the painting knife and brush with more delicacy — but it could be said, less radically — than Cézanne. The forest greens are built up in layers from different directions, allowing the superimposed paint, like a scumble, to be qualified by that beneath. Pissarro is also more concerned with recession, leading the eye back by means of the stream. For Cézanne much of the interest centres on the surface pattern of knife marks. Such a study might have been painted in situ on a painting expedition and then touched up in the studio.

PAUL CEZANNE
Etang des Soeurs, Osny
1875, Courtauld Institute Galleries, London

Cézanne in *Etang des Soeurs, Osny* (left), which was originally owned by Pissarro, uses the palette knife more rhythmically, unifying the painting with strong directional sweeps of the blade. After abandoning the palette knife, both artists eventually evolved a style of overall rhythmic strokes — Pissarro's juicy and shaped like a comma and Cézanne's more angular and constructivist.

1 *Actual size detail*

1 *Actual size detail* Perhaps under the influence of Cézanne, Pissarro's palette for this painting, although similar to that of earlier works with perhaps the addition of cadmium yellow, is used more boldly. In the central area of this painting, sizeable blocks of strong colour have been applied, skilfully capturing the fall of sunlight on the bridge and the reflections in the water. The bridge is a delicate merging of shades of ochre, working around a bright centre of cadmium yellow. The yellow patches of reflection in the water are made by touching the edge of the knife on the canvas and then smearing the paint down. This merges with a strong ultramarine blue reflection of the sky.

2 The very intricacy of the build-up of greens in the foliage contrasts with Cézanne's broader sweeps of paint. Here the juicy smears are qualified with delicate patches of glazes applied with the knife, tips of opaque paint and finally leaf-shaped dabs of the brush. The result is a rich area of texture and colour.

3 A patch of sunlight in a clearing leads the eye through the mid-ground screen of trees into the background. The tree-trunks have been built up with thick paint using the edge of the knife and the brush. But note how ridges of paint which catch the light define the contours of the stylized curves of these trunks.

2

3

Kitchen Garden with Trees in Flower, Pontoise

1877

$25^{3}/_{4} \times 31^{7}/_{8}$in/65.5×81cm

Oil on canvas

Musée d'Orsay, Paris

This celebration of springtime sees Pissarro, who was liable to bouts of melancholia, in a jubilant mood. One result of the experiments inspired by Cézanne in the mid-1870s was the emergence of a new style characterized by small, rhythmic strokes of thick paint, building up into areas of impasto. Here, in depicting the fruit trees in blossom, Pissarro appears to delight in the rich texture of the paint, dabbing on a brush tip loaded with white, then modifying it with green, ochre or blue.

In 1870 Pissarro's friend Ludovic Piette painted a *Portrait of Camille Pissarro Painting Outdoors,* in which the artist is shown standing before his easel with a small umbrella balanced over the canvas to stop the light reflecting off the wet paint. He is mixing his paints on his palette with a long-handled brush, and wears a broad-brimmed hat to shade his face from the sun. He would have painted this scene very much as Piette portrayed him. He liked to work standing up with his tripod easel anchored to the ground with a rock suspended from a piece of string from the apex. It is possible to imagine him at his work, constantly looking up at the scene he is painting before him, carefully observing each detail, until eventually, stroke by stroke, it is captured on the canvas. "One must always have only one master — nature," he warned a young artist. "She is the one always to be consulted."

The structure for the composition of this painting is one developed and explored by Pissarro mainly at the end of the 1870s. Through a screen of trees, which makes an interesting pattern in the foreground, the shapes of houses can be glimpsed in the background. Pissarro used this formula in many works painted around Pontoise at this time, including a river scene. It was a traditional theme explored by Daubigny and particularly Courbet in his forest scenes, but Pissarro — and indeed Monet and other members of the Impressionist group — were drawn to the abstract pattern made on the surface of the painting by a screen of trees, drawing the eye of the viewer into its depths and on to the scene beyond. Monet in similar scenes went on to abstract the screen of trees even further.

Pissarro's palette at the end of the 1870s narrows down perceptibly and the colours become purer. Yellow ochre is particularly evident in the paintings of this period. Here he emphasizes the horizontal swathe of ochre in the foreground and takes up the same colour in the blossom, the shutters of the house on the hill and also in the sky — in places quite strongly. The blue of the roofs, the rich green of the vegetables in the foreground and small dashes of a bright orange red are carried through the composition in the same way, but it is the bold application of the yellow — a warm colour which advances to the front of the picture — that helps to lead the eye round the painting.

Painted a few years after Pissarro's *Kitchen Garden,* the style is in many ways similar. Both artists build up the paint into a textured area of colours for the trees, treating the buildings behind more smoothly. "Look for the kind of nature that suits your temperament," Pissarro advised the young painter Le Bail. Certainly Pissarro shows here that he is still finding inspiration in aspects of the village of Pontoise. This painting demonstrates the early stages of an approach to painting with which he was to wrestle for his remaining years, and bears witness to a renewed interest in the texture of the paint surface prompted by his association with Cézanne. Even where the paint is thinner, as in the background and sky, the complex mesh of brushstrokes makes the paint surface shimmer with life and light. Here Pissarro, like Monet, builds up areas of colour and tone with separate touches of paint. This was, of course, the prescribed Impressionist method, but Pissarro here achieves his effects more through personal observation than by following a theory.

CLAUDE MONET
Springtime in Giverny
Private collection

1

2

1 In the background the buildings are skilfully contrived with a small brush with carefully observed strokes of colour. The paint, however, is smoothed out in contrast to the flurry of impasto dabs which make up the trees. As can be seen in this detail, the paint here is worked wet-in-wet but is barely one layer thick, permitting patches of the cream-primed canvas to show through to give a depth and unity to this area.

2 Focusing in on the brushstrokes that make up the flowering fruit trees, we can only marvel at the build-up of colour. Individual strokes of colour — sometimes surprisingly pure — are superimposed, mainly wet-in-wet. Notice how at this time the strokes are applied from all directions and, even though the paint appears thick, it does not cover the surface everywhere — small patches of bare canvas are visible in places.

3 *Actual size detail* Pissarro has captured the beauty of the blossom with what appears to be pure white. But in fact the dabs of white are rarely left pure as they are applied wet-in-wet so that the paint merges to some extent with the colour beneath. Also, Pissarro has modified the dry white in places with a thin layer of grey. When compared with the foreground row of cabbages in *The View of l'Hermitage* (see page 19), an increased subtlety of colour as well as a less pedestrian build-up of tone is apparent.

3 *Actual size detail*

Mme Pissarro Sewing Near a Window

1878-79

$21^1/_4 \times 17^3/_4$in/54×45cm

Oil on canvas

Ashmolean Museum, Oxford

A collection of Pissarro's portraits would make a delightful exhibition, showing us his loving family and a few close friends such as Cézanne. Although such paintings were informal ones, not painted for sale (indeed this portrait of Julie Pissarro remained in the family until bequeathed to the Ashmolean by her son Lucien), they were no less carefully conceived and executed. Pissarro, unlike his acquaintance Renoir, whose influence can be seen in this work, never painted society portraits. Instead, when times were lean, he signed on as a copyist at the Louvre, or painted signs, blinds and fans. Even at the ripe age of fifty-seven he sometimes had to sell watercolours for ten francs each, but his politics, not to mention his stubborn need to depict exactly what he saw, did not fit him for society portraiture. This touching portrait of his wife sewing anticipates his paintings of peasant women of the early 1880s, both in its treatment and in the enclosed setting.

In October 1878, Pissarro took a studio in the rue des Trois-Frères, Montmartre, where this portrait may have been painted. The couple's fourth son Ludovic-Rodolphe was born in Paris on 21 November, and it may be that Julie is heavily pregnant in this painting, which would explain the cursory execution of the lower area around the sewing. Pissarro explored this theme of a figure at the window many times, exploiting the *contre-jour* effect of the light and trying various ways of linking the figure in with the window frame. Here the bent head and torso are carefully placed in an enclosed space backed by the window and curtain. Pissarro has concentrated on surface pattern in this painting, preventing the eye from "looking out" through the window by blocking it with the decorative swirls of the wrought-iron balcony. Beyond this the scene is lightly painted, blurred and ambiguous. Consequently, attention is focused on the face through strong compositional lines such as the frame and cross bar of the window, cut by her head, the pattern of the wrought-iron, the line of her arm and the stripes of her dress. As in other compositions, Pissarro helps to unify the painting by repeating curves — in the ironwork, Julie's hand, her forehead and particularly her hair and the stray curls on the back of her head.

In the late 1870s Pissarro's paintings became more thickly worked, with areas of matted impasto. Here the figure is painted very densely, with the flesh tones constructed from superimposed strokes of strong colour — greens, blues and reds. This contrasts with the light treatment of the background and centre foreground, where an area of buff-primed canvas has been allowed to show through the sparse dry strokes of paint to represent the sewing fabric that Madame Pissarro is working on.

Standing back from this painting, the flesh tones glow and the figure achieves a remarkable sense of three-dimensionality. It is an intimate portrait that is full of light, outlining Julie Pissarro's profile and catching the highlights in her hair.

This painting, a small informal portrait of his wife Julie, is typical of Pissarro's style of the late 1870s. The paint surface in places has been built up into a web of small brushstrokes of colour to form a dense surface impasto. Understandably, at this time Pissarro became concerned that his paintings were overworked and lacking in clarity of form. Yet, as with this portrait, by standing back from the confusion of paint, the forms emerge clearly, standing out from the intended flatness of the background. In addition, the build-up of colour creates glowing flesh tones. The setting of the figure in an enclosed space (Pissarro takes positive steps to prevent the eye from straying out of the window with the wrought-iron balcony and the deliberate blurring of the scene outside — anticipates a persistent theme of the 1880s.

1

2

3

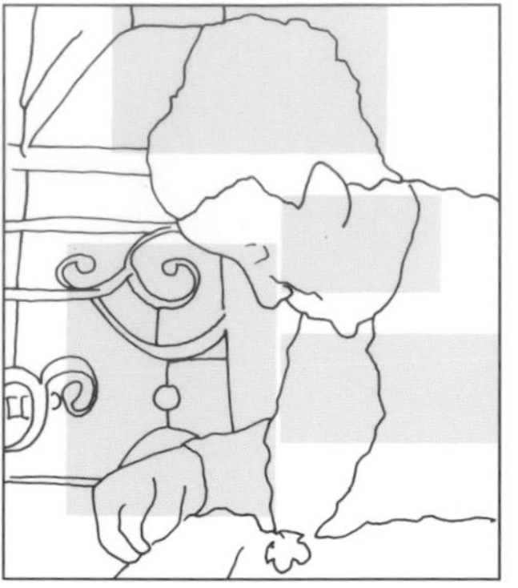

1 The basic mid-brown of the hair is created by a mass of individual brushstrokes lost in a mat of paint. Once dry, individual highlighted strands of hair have been carefully added, capturing the *contre-jour* fall of light. Note particularly the delicate vermilion highlights, probably added with a fine-pointed sable brush. Stray curls of hair on the back of Julie's bowed head reiterate the swirls of the wrought-iron balcony.

2 Like the hair, the face is loaded with tiny flecks of paint, often of pure colour – greens, blues, reds. Fine hatching strokes build up the colour in the ruddy cheeks with more blue and green in the shadow areas. The profile is highlighted by the *contre-jour* light from the window.

3 The expressive brushwork marking the fluid stripes of the bodice and following the contours of the folds and the form of the body creates an area of movement in the painting. Creamy impasto highlights are built up where the sun streams in through the window.

4 *Actual size detail* Here the thick build-up of flesh tones on the hand contrasts with the thin dry strokes of paint dragged over the buff-coloured primed canvas which shows through to represent the fabric Madame Pissarro is sewing. The finely woven canvas, which has a strong diagonal weave, shows up well. Pissarro has painstakingly blended the tiny touches of paint to describe the form.

4 *Actual size detail*

THE SHEPHERDESS

1881
$31^7/_8 \times 25^1/_2$in/81×64.7cm
Oil on canvas
Musée d'Orsay, Paris

Like other members of the Impressionist group, Pissarro, by the end of the 1870s, had become dissatisfied with his work and sought to introduce a more structured method to his painting. Perhaps in an effort to simplify the content of his compositions, he turned from the spatial problems inherent in landscape painting to portrait-like representations of peasant girls. These figures were usually set in an enclosed space, often against a backdrop of stylized foliage like that in *The Shepherdess.* During the early 1880s Pissarro concentrated on this theme, depicting peasants – mostly girls – talking, eating, working the land or, as in the case of *The Shepherdess,* just thinking. Although to the modern eye these peasant portraits appear more idealized and therefore more romantic than his work to date, at the time they were regarded as showing life at its most base.

Even in his earliest drawings, Pissarro showed a fascination for the everyday dreary drudge of peasant life. He loved the clamour of the market place and the dockside, drawing and painting the black cargo handlers in St Thomas and later the Indians in Caracas. In the countryside outside Paris, he found other, less picturesque, peasant tasks worthy of his attention – such as women digging, weeding or washing dishes. It is not surprising that he found his ideas in tune with Anarchist ideology which upheld the work of the peasant – in harmony with nature and shared by others – as the ideal.

In his peasant girl paintings, Pissarro concentrates on the facial features and the detailing of the clothing, focusing on the character of the person. *The Shepherdess* is a simple country girl, idling on a shady bank, but there is more to her than this: she is young and pretty and is shown in a wistful, rather sad mood. Some would say she was reflecting on the misery of her lot but Pissarro, with typical bourgeois misconception, would have seen her life as ideal. Pissarro's work of this time is often compared with that of Jean-François Millet. But although Millet also studied peasants at work, his paintings commenting on their plight, he did not have the same approach to realism as Pissarro, who saw the peasants as people rather than as symptoms of a social malady. Pissarro's peasant pictures are closer in conception to the figure paintings of Renoir and Degas. Pissarro was working with Degas in his studio in 1879, collaborating on a printing project, and it is possible that Degas' portrait-like studies of dancers at work inspired him, as his own were later to inspire Gauguin.

At the seventh Impressionist Exhibition of 1882 Pissarro exhibited thirty paintings, most of them figure studies, which were particularly admired by the influential critic J. K. Huysmans. But it was a different story the following year when *The Shepherdess* was exhibited in London by the dealer Durand-Ruel with ten other paintings by Pissarro and works by Renoir, Sisley, Morisot, Cassatt, Degas, Monet and Manet. Despite the rantings of outraged critics, who thought Pissarro's work uncouth and unfinished, Lucien encouraged his father to exhibit again. "Alas, I shall never do more careful, more finished work," he lamented.

Pissarro's execution of *The Shepherdess* shows a development in his painting style from that of the late 1870s. The consistent comma-like brushstroke, formerly restricted to certain areas of the painting, now delicately fuses the picture surface, locking the figure into the background. Each area is built up from small strokes of colour, sometimes worked wet-in-wet into the brushstrokes below to modify them, sometimes carefully placed alongside. In this way he captures the dappled sunlight playing on the pensive figure. The almost classical treatment of this figure in its solidity of form, dignity and general restraint combined with what was considered the base nature of the subject matter proved a tantalizing combination for the younger generation of artists in Paris (and in particular Gauguin) whom it was to influence greatly.

1

2

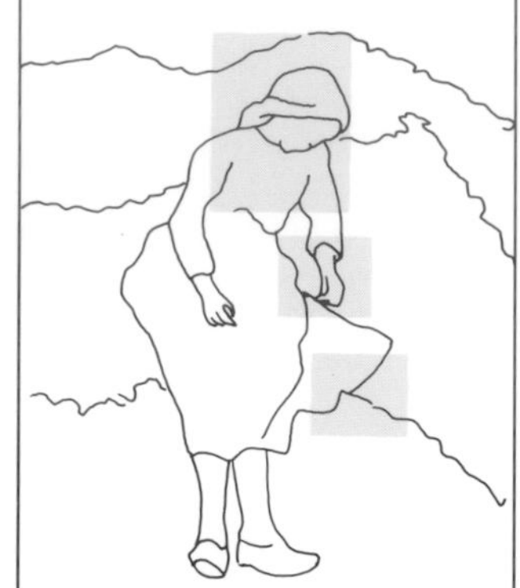

1 The glorious confluence of the painted background can be fully appreciated in this detail. A wide mixture of hues – sometimes pure greens, yellows, reds, blues and blacks – are worked over and into each other. In places the dried impasto of an earlier layer appears contrary when superimposed on a thin stroke of colour in another direction, but the result is a living area of paint of infinite depth.

2 Pissarro seems to dwell on the girl's overlarge peasant hands, but it is quite likely that he admired them. Streaks of blue reflected from her skirt form the shadows on her fingers, whereas on her wrist the shadow is blacker, picking up the colour of her shirt.

3 *Actual size detail* Pissarro is known to have kept a number of paintings going at the same time, allowing one to dry while working on another. In this way he could develop the exact colour or tone he was seeking by working with wet paint on the dried surface below. Here the small hatched layers of strokes, crossing over one another to form a dense layer of paint, create a sense of solid form. However, the brushstrokes here, unlike those seen in his earlier work, do not describe the outline of the form but rather the play of light on it.

3 *Actual size detail*

The Quays at Rouen

1883

$18^{1}/_{4} \times 22$in/46.3×55.7cm

Oil on canvas

Courtauld Institute Galleries, London

Pissarro's visit to the city of Rouen in October 1883 was very important to him. It gave him a new perspective on life which inspired a large number of oil paintings, watercolours, drawings and later etchings. This first visit may have been inspired by Monet's paintings of the façade of Rouen Cathedral of 1872, or it may have been encouraged by Pissarro's patron Eugène Murer, the Paris *restaurateur* and pastry chef, who befriended many of the Impressionists, and in whose hotel in Rouen Pissarro stayed. Murer, by enticing the hard-up painters with his delicious food, had by the end of the 1870s collected many fine paintings including twenty-five by Pissarro.

Having concentrated on landscapes and the lives of country people up to this time, Pissarro's work from this first visit to Rouen, of which thirteen paintings survive, was to anticipate the major theme of the last twenty years of his life. These were scenes of Rouen, Paris, Le Havre and Dieppe painted from the seclusion and shelter of an upstairs hotel room. This busy scene on the Seine, with barges lining the banks, loading and unloading their cargo, and smoking dock chimneys in the background, is typical of his later work. It is possible that the subject matter appealed to him as it related to his earliest drawings of cargo handlers in the port of Charlotte Amalie.

Unlike his intimate studies of country peasants painted at about this time, these descriptive paintings show his desire to remain aloof from the busy workings of the town. In contrast to Renoir's close-up figure paintings, showing Parisians at leisure and play, Pissarro's townscapes are populated with dark, faceless people — sometimes close to caricature — pursuing lives of drab monotony, many with the stooping shoulders of the world-weary.

In this painting, Pissarro comes close to perfecting the style of repetitive brushwork towards which he was working in the late 1870s. The picture surface is alive with closely worked small brushstrokes, yet in no place does the surface become overworked and muddied, as in some of his paintings of this period. The painting's unity is achieved firstly through the consistency of the brushwork over the surface and secondly by colour, particularly dashes of strong viridian green and yellow ochre. There is much here that points towards Pissarro's imminent and radical change in style under the influence of the Neo-Impressionists. But his use of a consistent small brushstroke and pure colour, always nascent in his work, shows that his style did not in fact have to change as fundamentally to accommodate their science-based theories as is sometimes supposed.

Writing to his son Lucien from Rouen in November, Pissarro expresses self-doubts. "I have just concluded my series of paintings. I keep looking at them. I who created them often find them terrible. I understand them only at rare moments." But not long afterwards he writes in a more positive mood. "Result of my trip: I return with pleasure to my studio and look over my studies with greater indulgence with a better idea of what needs to be done to them." In *Bouquet of Flowers,* painted in 1898, Pissarro places this painting in the background, which shows he liked it enough to hang it, but also that it had not been popular with potential buyers.

This scene of the quays at the cathedral city of Rouen was one of a series marking a new direction in Pissarro's work which was to absorb him fully in his later years. Painting unobserved from the upstairs window of a hotel room, he was able to make visual comments on the busy interchange of dock life. This bird's-eye view was in direct contrast to the closer viewpoint of his peasant girl "portraits" of the same time. The composition is divided into four horizontal areas of sky, hill, river and road, broken with incidental verticals — chimneys, lamp posts, masts, figures and the strongly realized building on the right. The composition is unified, however, through the consistent brushwork over the whole surface of the painting. In addition, patches of white smoke and bright colour throughout the painting — viridian, yellow and vermilion in particular — help to integrate the disparate elements. Pissarro has cleverly broken up the expanse of road in the foreground with the shadow of a church spire and building out of the picture — a compositional device he was fond of.

1

2

1 On the far bank of the river, the flat barges and belching factory chimneys contribute to the type of scene admired by Pissarro. Here the hues are reduced in strength with the addition of white, but the brushwork is no less lively.

2 The horse and cart and the small family group alongside, are skilfully portrayed, with admirable economy. Pissarro omits all unnecessary detail — the cart appears to have only one wheel and the horse no reins. Yet the eye fills in this information.

3 *Actual size detail* As if to draw attention to what might seem an insignificant part of the composition, Pissarro carefully explores the nuances of the shadow on the street corner. The deft brushstrokes, which appear to have been laid on with a small soft-haired brush, create a vibrant surface, while the road traffic is created with larger, more confident strokes — in higher contrast and more detail in the foreground than in the background. To emphasize the sense of recession, Pissarro has built up the foreground with layers of increasingly small strokes of strong colour. In the background, the paint is more thinly applied and in bolder strokes.

3 *Actual size detail*

The Boulevard Montmartre at Night

1897
$20^{3}/_{4} \times 25^{1}/_{2}$in/53×65cm
Oil on canvas
National Gallery, London

Although living and working in the countryside for most of his life, Pissarro kept a studio in Paris when he could afford it. However, with a few exceptions, he showed no interest in the city as a subject for painting until the last twenty years of his life. It seems that the visit to Rouen in 1883 (see page 46) captured his imagination and, when in 1888 he contracted an eye infection which obliged him to reconsider his working methods, he decided to turn his attention to a study of urban themes. He had always considered painting from nature *(en plein air)* of the greatest significance to his art, but his eye was sensitive to both light and cold, particularly wind. This meant that except on warm still days he had to work from the shelter of an interior, and finding such a room, with a view that could sustain his interest, led him back to the city. Monet also painted scenes of Waterloo Bridge from the Savoy Hotel in London in his old age.

Typically, Pissarro tackled his new-found subject with great enthusiasm, writing to Lucien in 1897: "I am delighted to be able to paint these Paris streets that people have come to call ugly, but which are so silvery, so luminous and vital." But he did not restrict himself to views in Paris; he also spied down from hotel windows on the lively streets and ports of Rouen, Dieppe and Le Havre, and painted many of the scenes depicted by the Impressionists in their early years. He even took up early Impressionist themes as well, studying the effect of weather and passing time in series of paintings, as Monet was doing at much the same time.

In early 1897 Pissarro established himself in the Grand Hôtel de Russie, Paris, close to his old studio in rue des Trois-Frères. Here, working from an upstairs room, he painted thirteen views of the Boulevard Montmartre (and later made a lithograph), showing it in different weather conditions and at different times of day, but only once at night. Here he captures in bold brushstrokes of colour the fashionable life of this busy street on a wet night, the road a pattern of luminous greys and blues; and the pavement reflecting the lights of the cafés and restaurants.

For Pissarro these late urban themes solved one of the overriding problems of his early landscapes — that of depicting recession. The architectural structure of a Paris street gave his paintings a natural spatial depth, leaving him free to concentrate on other aspects of the painting. Here he leads the eye into the dark void with lines of dancing lights — the street lamps, the lines of carriages and the watery reflections on the pavements. He enforces the receding lines of the street and buildings with tonal extremes — dark shadows and bright lights — and eliminates the detail of the boulevard buildings, even reducing the picturesque skyline of the rooftops on the right to a harsh black line.

In the last two prolific decades of his life Pissarro suffered from a recurring eye infection and was forced to paint inside. But the formula he had discovered in Rouen in 1883 of painting city life from the seclusion of an upstairs room continued to prove a source of inspiration. Like other members of the Impressionist group, notably Monet, Pissarro took to painting series of a single scene in different weather conditions. In 1897 he painted a series of the Boulevard Montmartre from a room in the Grand Hôtel de Russie. This lively night scene – the only one in his *oeuvre* – is more like an oil sketch than the others in the series, which are painted in the dense impasto typical of his later years; he seems to have worked quickly in an attempt to capture the lights and silvery reflections in the wet street before they disappeared.

1 *Actual size detail*

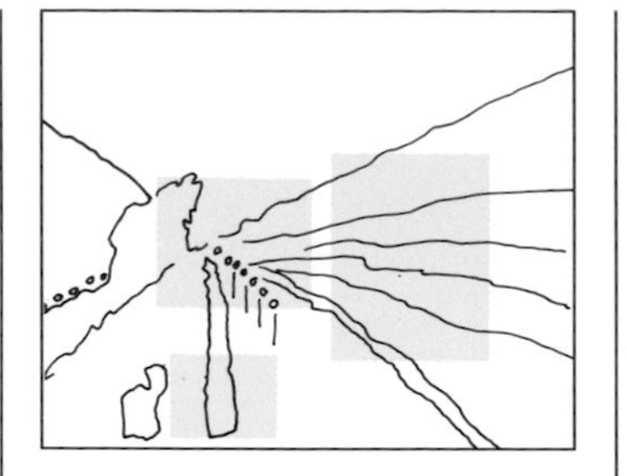

1 *Actual size detail* Pissarro seems to have battled with this perverse street lamp — it dominates the foreground of twelve of his thirteen views of the boulevard. (In his crowd-packed vision of the street at *mardi-gras*, he takes the unprecedented step of omitting it for "cosmetic" reasons.) The build-up of impasto and the surrounding circle of light draws the eye to the centre of the canvas, to survey the scene in its entirety. The bright lights of night-time Paris are boldly expressed in vertical strokes of juicy paint.

2 Pissarro was always concerned with recession into the picture space, and here the paint is in general more thinly applied in the background. The exception is the thick impasto of the street lamps, which help the illusion of space by leading the eye into it. The pulsating area of deep violet blue where the lines of the street converge also helps to draw the eye into the picture.

3 The silvery reflection of light on the wet surface of the boulevard is created with a scumble of pale blue over a layer of interwoven flat strokes of pinky browns. A few carefully placed strokes of colour describe the line of oncoming carriages.

2

3

Apple Picking at Eragny-sur-Epte

1888

$23^1/_2 \times 28^3/_4$in/60×73cm

Oil on canvas

Museum of Fine Art, Dallas

Apple Picking at Eragny-sur-Epte is one of Pissarro's most successful Neo-Impressionist paintings. In it, he has succeeded in capturing with a luminosity of colour the diffused, hazy light of high summer. It is no wonder that in 1885 he said of his earlier work: "I find them poor, tame, grey, monotonous." By 1888, Pissarro and his family were established at Eragny-sur-Epte, not far from Monet at Giverny. He was to live in this farmhouse for the rest of his life, buying it in 1892 with a loan of 15,000 francs (soon repaid) from Monet. In his letters to Lucien, Pissarro jests about "Eragny Castle," and talks of Julie's pride in her flower garden, but to Pissarro it was a never-ceasing source of inspiration for his work.

Pissarro's meeting in 1895 with Seurat and Signac was to have a radical effect on his art. Like many of the Impressionists, he had been searching for new inspiration which would take his work beyond their early theories. A feeling of stagnancy after the heady years of innovation had turned Renoir to the rediscovery of classical roots and Degas to experiments with different media. Pissarro too had been making progress towards a formulation of his style, and Seurat's theories based on the scientific integration of tone, colour and line seemed like a natural progression from his own work. The application of the paint in small dots of pure colour, known as Pointillism, was a refinement of his painting style of the early 1880s, and the theories on "mixing" the colours optically on the canvas developed and formalized his own exploration. Even the Neo-Impressionist formula for landscape, with the curved horizon, uptilted ground and generalized, atmospheric indication of recession, led on from Pissarro's "peasant girl" backdrops.

It was during the 1880s and 1890s that Pissarro's radical political sympathies hardened, culminating in his overt support of the Anarchist movement. In Seurat and Signac, he found fellow Anarchists, whose political leanings were expressed in their new theories, which led to their rejection by the rest of the Impressionist group. Pissarro supported their inclusion in the group exhibition of 1885, which caused Monet and Renoir to refuse to participate. The anonymity of the Pointillist dot, which removed the "signature" of a painter's brushmark or style, in theory worked towards the creation of artists' cooperatives, where paintings would appear similar in style and could be sold under the name of the cooperative rather than that of the individual artist. Pissarro explained that "originality consists solely in the character of the drawing and the vision of each artist." Even though the expressive brushwork of the Impressionists was scorned by the Neo-Impressionists as being romantic, Seurat and Pissarro, in particular, soon found this curbing of individuality hard to bear. Pissarro was in every way excited by the theory, but, in practice, he found it laborious and time-consuming as well as alien to the sensitivities of nature that he wished to capture in paint. In addition, he had lost many of his carefully nurtured patrons and found it hard to sell his work, which undoubtedly prompted his return to his former style.

The orchard of Pissarro's farmhouse in Eragny, and particularly the harvesting of the apples, were subjects to which Pissarro returned throughout the last years of his life. For this particular version, painted using the Pointillist method of the Neo-Impressionists, Pissarro, unusually, made several careful preparatory drawings and also an oil sketch and a gouache. The gouache shows that he considered placing a fifth figure where the basket now stands on the right, but he substituted the horse and cart in the background at the last moment. Pissarro found the Pointillist method very stifling but during his brief flirtation with Neo-Impressionism he painted some remarkable canvases of exceptional luminosity.

Camille Pissarro
Study of the Orchard at Eragny-sur-Epte
1885-90, Ashmolean Museum, Oxford

This sketchbook study in black chalk of the distinctive gnarled tree included in *Apple Picking* is one of a number of preparatory works for the painting, which include an oil sketch and a gouache. In the final painting Pissarro changed his viewpoint of the tree, standing back from it and looking up at the foliage like the pickers themselves. He also chose to sharpen the angled distortion of the trunk, reiterating the angle in the bent arms of the pickers.

1

2

3

1 This detail from the background shows how the colours here have been considerably tinted with white both to emulate the bleaching effect of the hazy atmosphere and strong sunlight and to imply a sense of distance.

2 Even though he tried to adhere to the theory of the Neo-Impressionists, Pissarro found it difficult to subject himself to the limitations of the Pointillist dot. This figure is constructed with a fine cross-hatched stroke, emphasizing the contours of the body. But he uses pure strokes of colour, as prescribed, to build up the form with yellow highlights from the sun's rays and blue reflections from the sky in the shadows.

3 This detail of the shadowed area under the tree shows both the regularity of Pissarro's "dot," and his careful adherence to the recommended Neo-Impressionist palette. The shadow colour is given a vibrancy through the juxtaposition of complementary colours – reds and greens, and violets and yellows. The patches of dappled sunlight have been stippled over the shadow colours. The Neo-Impressionists recommended the use of chalk and glue to prime their canvases, which gave a whiter, more matt and absorbent surface to work on. They found that allowing small patches to show through the brushwork, as Pissarro has done here, added to the overall luminosity of the painting.

4 *Actual size detail*

4 *Actual size detail* Visible in this detail is the dilute painted outline mapping out the composition, which is not quite obliterated by the superimposed strokes of paint. It appears that thin washes of tone were roughly laid in before the strokes of colour were placed.

SELF-PORTRAIT

1903

$16^1/_8 \times 13^1/_8$in/41×33.3cm

Oil on canvas

Tate Gallery, London

Even in the last years of his life Pissarro never lost the impetus to work. "Work is a wonderful regulator of mind and body. In the joy of working, I forget all sorrow, grief, bitterness, I even ignore them," he said. So for this dignified self-portrait, which turned out to be his last, it is appropriate that he shows himself seated at the window of his Paris studio at 28 Place Dauphine, behind him the busy streets of the city which inspired the paintings of his last years.

Pissarro seems to have made no concessions to his old age. He spent each summer of his last years painting the docks from hotel windows; in 1901 and 1902 in Dieppe, in 1903 in Le Havre. He was as active selling his paintings as he was painting them, withholding the whole of his Dieppe series from his dealer Durand-Ruel when he found that the latter was conspiring with the Bernheim Jeune gallery to keep the prices down. In the summer of 1903 he sold two canvases to the Museum at Le Havre. By this time Pissarro had found acceptance, and his work was sufficiently highly regarded for forgeries to be on the market, signed with an inaccurate "Pissaro." His work had found its way into more respected museums; Gustave Caillebotte, an amateur painter and great organizer of the Impressionist exhibitions, bequeathed on his death his fine collection of Impressionists to the Musée du Luxembourg in Paris, who were unwilling to accept it. After a heated debate, they were exhibited in 1897, in effect the first public showing of the work of the Impressionists.

In October 1898 Pissarro travelled to Amsterdam, where he viewed the Rembrandt exhibition. It is possible that he drew inspiration from the self-portraits of the ageing artist, particularly in the attitude of the sitter, who seeks the attention of the viewer but at the same time remains aloof. Pissarro painted three self-portraits in these last years, and in addition was sculpted by the dentist-sculptor Paulin, and it is tempting to believe that he was motivated by similar feelings to those of Rembrandt's dignified elderly sitter Jacob Trip, who had his portrait painted at least six times, it is thought in an effort to provide as many as possible of his twelve children with something to remember him by.

Pissarro appears a little frail in this last portrait, but the glint in his eye is evidence of his unquenchable spirit. Here we see Pissarro the patriarch, as perhaps he wished his children to remember him: upright with a steady look, his white beard flowing over his chest. As in his portrait of Julie (page 38), he takes advantage of the window setting and the *contre-jour* light which forms strong contrasts, as well as the compositional arrangement offered by the frame, which breaks up the background.

The view through the window, seen in reverse as it is painted from the reflection in a mirror, is of the houses on the site of the present Samaritaine by the Pont Neuf. It is painted in muted, soft colours, in contrast to the dark interior, but the blurred image does not take attention away from the sitter.

Pissarro has executed this self-portrait with confidence and a facility which barely indicates his age. Except for the face and areas of impasto highlighting, the paint is applied in thin dabs, allowing small areas of the greyish primed canvas to show through. The winter coat and wide-brimmed hat, in which Pissarro was also sculpted by Paulin, is built up in superimposed brushstrokes of black, with blue and green, and even red.

This touching self-portrait, executed in Pissarro's Paris studio at 28 Place Dauphine in the last months of his life, bears witness to his strength of purpose — at the grand age of seventy-three he was still painting continuously. His piercing eyes, here shown peering over his half-moon glasses, were evidently no less observant, and the precise and delicate brushwork is a testimony to the steadiness of his hands. The marvellous build-up of the flesh tones with carefully placed strokes of pure colour and the precise placing of highlights demonstrate the facility and confidence with which he was painting at this time.

1

2

1 The strong outline of the first mapping out of the composition visible along the shoulder line shows Pissarro's confident grip. His coat is built up from a flat layer of dark grey stippled over with a darker layer of dabs with a flat hog's hair brush. Accents of vermilion and ultramarine spike this potentially dull area of black.

2 Through the window, the houses of the present Samaritaine by the Pont Neuf are viewed in reverse, as painted in a mirror. By sketching them in muted, bleached colours, Pissarro has ensured that attention is not drawn away from the commanding portrait.

3 *Actual size detail* Areas of flat tone have been laid in on the face and then built up with delicate parallel strokes – mixtures of vermilion, white, umber and ochre combined on the palette. The paint appears to have been diluted with medium except for the impasto highlights and the delicate lines of dark brown added with a very fine brush to delineate the features. Pissarro's bushy beard, which turned grey when he was forty-three, is cleverly conceived in layers of sparse dabs to evoke a sense of volume without substance. Except in a few strokes round the mouth and on the coat, Pissarro avoids the more obvious linear conception of the beard.

3 *Actual size detail*

Index

Page numbers in *italic* refer to illustrations and captions

PHOTOGRAPHIC CREDITS

The photographs in this book were provided by the following: Ashmolean Museum, Oxford 11-14, 15 top, 27-29, 39-41, 55 bottom; Bridgeman Art Library, London 15 bottom, 23, 31-33, 35 bottom, 55-57;Courtauld Institute Galleries 23-25, 31 bottom, 47-49; Hubert Josse, Paris 6, 10, 35 top, 36-37, 43-45; National Gallery, London 7-9, 51-53; Tate Gallery, London 59-61; Wallraf-Richartz Museum, Cologne 19-21.